The Book of Venus

Plumalia Henson

Plumalia Henson
plumaliapress@gmail.com

ISBN 979-8-9889899-9-8 (trade paperback)

First Printing, November 2024

Printed in the United States of America.

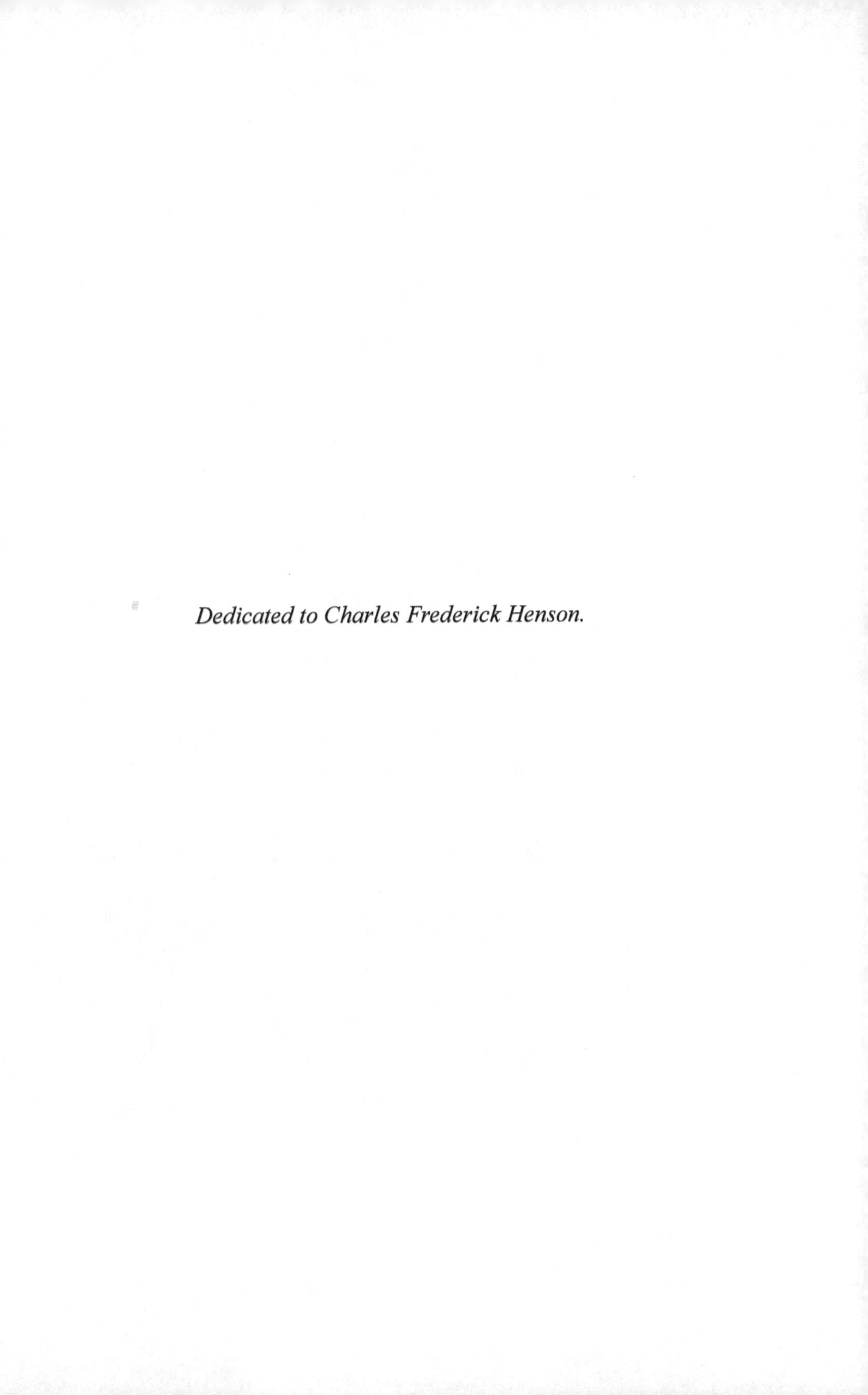

Dedicated to Charles Frederick Henson.

The Book of Venus

Plumalia Henson

i hate you.
no you don't, you say.
you hate the idea of me;
the idea of a patriarchal figure holding a place in your heart.

you're wrong.
i'm never wrong, you declare
with such a confidence-
that i never was taught.
there are different shades of right,
but i am never wrong.

if i could kill you bloodlessly-
but you could never do that.

if i could-
why simmer over hypotheticals?
why let mere possibilities consume you?
why so weak?
why so angry?
why?

i hate you.

i knew you would.

i am so serenely beautiful so totally and completely wanted
and nobody you have ever met has had these perfect
little stars placed so delicately in their eyes as i
i am wonderful and kind and protected by the moon
in which she holds me always underneath her billowing gaze
between my curtains as i sigh my bones away
and cry on my floor because nobody ever looks at me
and she goes
wow.
you are a darling creation.
i am so dissatisfied with my twelfth life
and how it has left me-
swimming alone in the pool
staring at the beautiful moonstone tile and wondering
when people say i am so pretty
do they mean it?
or is it their acknowledgement
of my unrelenting
godforsaken womanhood
their validation of my secondary sex?
or perhaps
they think i am beautiful,
and that is why they reach so deep into me like starving hands
reaching into the softest marshmallow depths of a warm july
sunrise

i was once perfect like you said.
i had not yet been laid to waste among these hands and teeth
that claw and gnaw and bite and take and take and take
thieving fingers.
i want our souls to become properly homogenous when the
moon rises

and she will finally glance at my fresh-bleached bedding with
that piercing gaze
and smile to find it empty.

this is it
the very last time
the final exorbitant display of affection i can hardly bear
that i claw from mine own organs
and smear on the wall
because i
am a full heart
an angel of love
and the only one.
it will never leave me
those sickening associations in your mind
it is inside me still,
for it knows that it is all that i have.

i looked at those miniature displays
and couldn't help but put my hand inside the chest
and imagine a tiny heart beating there
i felt it in my eyes, then
a vein bursting and dripping and seeping down my sinuses
though my mind felt so dry
heartbreak and panic
so much panic.
time will not heal this pain
it is etched into my bones.

dear god,
let me get prettier in his eyes with time.
let me age like a viciously tart raspberry wine
let me never stop being delicate and kind
no matter how the boot prints line
my shoulders
no matter how my skin cracks and peels and glows from
crying
i can deserve this.
i can be the thing i long for
i will be the one meant for me.

i can thin my blood until it runs like spring water
so it may never rise to fill my head
and clot my mind with horrific thoughts of what i could have
what i should have
what i may continue to be.

innocent
purged
the blood,
to wash from my hands
the yelling,
to cease.

pretty in
a gentle way
cradled
like a baby.
redeemed.

but
the horror
to mean something.
to make the clean feel clean
after surviving the dirt.

sometimes the bruises sprout from my bones
without a cause
infernal memories
that make me so sore sick i can't stand to
feel how my ribs stretch to make room for breath
or raise my arms to wash my hair
but i beg for you
to find the time
where you sit next to me and your leg touches mine in that
slight way
so we feel that little sparkle beneath the skin
creating a newborn star in us.
centimeters or feet or miles
or years, if you can believe in them
are so horribly untouchable in this humid room
where all my tears soak the walls
soak my skin
until i am ready to be heartbroken again.

i have realized something
the love i have for you is an endless fount
unconditional, unwavering, unrelenting love
i love you in every way you allow me to
and i find that who you are
captivates me
cages me
soothes me
turns me into the red-mouthed animal
i always felt i was
i love you
because you give my homesickness a home
a doorstep for the birds i catch
a bed to grow tired for
a pair of arms to wrap myself in
no longer am i soaked in chilling sweat
tears that pour from a tap shoved straight through the heart
for in you finding me, i found you
and now i have turned to religion
so i can pray for both of our souls
to never find ourselves apart

agony
agony
agony haunts me
the way a lover would
with those hands that taunt me when i begin to fall asleep
with that heart that beats ferociously against my ear until i can
no longer hear my own
i stop,
look, and find agony
listen, and hear it in me
feel the shivering that never will cease
i die today
so why am i still alive?
if the heart no longer beats
and the body no longer feeds
the empty tissue that resides
has already moved on to the afterlife
why am i still alive?
why can't i seem to die?
if the body inside my body has died,
why can't i?

i wish feeling lighter didn't feel like losing myself
and my fires fading didn't resemble the death of an old
childhood friend
all those nights spent crying hadn't turned into an empty,
medicated,
satiated
pit;
but it is good to move on
good to continue living
even if i miss dearly the comfort of the pain,
or the ache of the hurt.
it is better now.
we can be better,
now.
it does not shrivel my skin any longer to hear that word-
a ghost that whispers in your ear
it is time to leave it behind.
let it all go,
exhale it out into the humid midnight haze
and bury that devastating little girl for good.

when his lips parted
and a soul clawed a path through the gaps in his teeth
i bet it was beautiful
his bones creamy white
and perfectly articulated
thin,
though his skin may have been
it was tough.

i hope when the dirt dissolves you within it
it feels like the hug i always wanted to give you
i loved you so much
it was all consuming

i remember driving home
that deer jumping in front of your car
and i could have said something about the hesitation in your
hands
but i was scared
always so consumed by fear
loud noise around me swallowing as i trickled down
subdued
afraid
small.
i thought about your carelessness for life
and how it directly dueled my diamond view of you
and i wondered
i still wonder
if the point of my gaze
the lock of my eyes
was the rope around your throat
keeping you from becoming a heart-eating, home-wrecking,
blood-letting natural disaster.
if my big eyes watching you made bile fill your throat;
if my fingertips made you itch.
i let you into the softest parts of me
for a moment
and awoke to barbs in my shoes by the door

we kissed on the mouth
it was enchanting
you tasted of rust and salt
like the ocean
so i asked if you had been crying again
i tasted bloody
like a victim
and you asked if i had been biting again
so we walked down the empty street
hand in shivering hand
never again prying
for fear of being pried apart

every day the string loosens around my pinky finger
and every day my pants fall a little lower around my waist
i am diminishing
releasing everything
shedding
no control, nothing holding me back from simply
losing everything
especially when everything was never that much
no gods fawn over my angled face
nobody to grab my shoulders when i choke on my own rotted
saliva
from the excess of conditions for my existing
but i will always re-knot the string
and get new jeans
though everything is still so ugly
and the sky hasn't been blue in years
all that encircles my mind as a halo
is the sweet, sugary departure awaiting me at every uncertain
angle
but if i were to free my eyes
with what jagged fingernail remains i wouldn't be able to see
things changed
so i suppose better is not so bad a word
to walk into the unknown with all my heart
than to sit in the woods and wait for an echo to call my name

why am i begging?
begging for what-
to be looked at?
to be read so delicately
with tender care applied to the breakability of my spine?
to be listened to
actually listened to, not just begrudgingly heard
why do i crawl through this gravel and fire and glass
for a flower and a note
why has my vocabulary been weakened
reduced to a string of pleases
why can i not be framed and hung?

there is something in that boy
in his static gaze, how shocking
in his smile, layers upon layers of my dead skin tucked
like bolts of silk
between his teeth
he did pull those needles from my fingertips
swallowed them
an adam's apple-
a pincushion
seamstress's hands in the way he rearranged those incendiary
bits in my mind
surrounding me with the books i devoured in my teenaged
years
save for the loneliness of a determined last page
there is something terrifying in that man
he kissed me
that,
i did not request
ask or plead or beg for
i did not mastermind this transaction or request a
metamorphosis
to be stilled and calmed
i never did ask for you

you are not ugly
you are just beautiful in a way they cannot comprehend
you are not impulsive-
you are secretive around those who boast knowing your
erratic heart rhythm
everything about you has been suckled from your fingers
without question
identified without explanation
you are not hard to love.
you are a wounded animal, bleeding
in places people do not yearn to see
in spots nobody fantasizes about kissing
you are everybody's soulmate
and they will remember you when they reach their twelfth
life's end
and reach to hold you in those final breaths.
you are not afraid of love

you can only truly cry that mangled cry from your soul once
your mind will learn to close those doors so swiftly
will learn to refuse to return to
a gargling scream that alters your very being in its
construction
she said the moment is like a ghost that never leaves you
and i think about that all of the damn time

awash in morning sun and lazy rain
drink from the hands of your lover
such small and sweet hands kept so soft
never to scratch or kick or bite
decadent stillness embroidered into the kitchen towels

someday is so far
so many more than three-hundred and sixty-five days in a
year
far fewer than twenty-four hours in a day
but those same hands hold all that the universe could bear to
inherit you
waiting for when you are ready
the softest bonfire blanket you ever have been swaddled in

that girlish spring has come and gone
a sticky, sugary grape juice
evaporated under the cruel and cancerous
dry sunlight
more unrelenting every year
as the cicadas grow quieter, the colors dull
the hours turn to seconds turn to grains of sand to dust to
nothing
twisting and weaving into your scalp and out of reach of your
unbitten fingernails
it must be a woman's curse
for i felt like such a sunflower at eleven years old
and i shoot in reverse into the dirt
with every passing moment
scorned youth neatly organized into three young girls
encircling you in the weeds with those red ribbons
as you sleep with heavier and heavier eyes
cry in quieter, hushed tones
refuse yourself honeysuckle and bare feet
for the sake of maturity
still, a precious child will always remain
and i will cradle her in my grave

i kept your secrets
runs along the tubes
echoes through the machines
i kept your secrets
they were mine to wander through and dream of
deep kisses in my bedroom against the golden light
runs along the tubes
screams down the halls
i kept your secrets
i could face myself every day with the weight of my heart
outlined in my eyes
but you could not bear it
i knew you didn't ask
another weight to sprain you
another dragging presence lost to guiding you
i kept your secrets
even through the tubes
and the crying flatline
with only those to keep me company.

oh my god if you
if you said
just said that you
that you could even begin to feel sorry
even plan to sketch a naked apology
i would forgive you
so
damn
fast
but you don't say anything to me anymore
and that only leaves more devastating hurt to be
apologized for

there was a knife that glittered so fiercely
held to my throat
and nobody else could see it but you
i am getting better.
i am getting better.
it said i am getting better.
but it was an instrument in my suffering
my masochistic itch that burned
like hot grease corroding my integument
the stitches in my psyche are tangled to each other in the dirt,
now
the cracks in my teeth deepen
widening
opening ferociously in all directions
eyelashes and fingernails and chunks of skin and hair and
bone ease through as though i have finally understood-
i have no one to be pretty for.
as day to day has birthed a new routine
consciousness to consciousness like a television screen
flipping through alternatives of how it could have gone
how i could have decorated myself to be received
more entirely
more politely by you
not perfect
just quieter than before.

i imagined cherubic hallucinations in my bathtub
flying in dizzying circles around me, whispering
godforsaken whispering
things i never could quite hope to hear
with the faint echo of joints clicking in and out of place to
punctuate
every shallow breath

i imagined perfection for two minutes-
maybe three
that disgusting mechanism
abhorrent third mind above mine
indistinguishable from the cream porcelain entombing what
once was only my body
but now is communally managed

i imagined a tremendous storm came out of me
it burned away my hair and flung the skin from my bones and
frayed my muscles
every thought of my existence turned to a silken ash beneath
my feet that i could swallow and finally digest
until all that remained in the spotless world
were my eyes
and i still used them to search for you
always one to mistake a warning for a welcome

do you think
in the blood red childbirthing of the first daughter
the first mother stretched her fingers to her side
and found herself unable to comprehend why she could yearn
so incredibly for an
emptiness yet to be described
was she jealous of her own daughter as she brushed her hair
before ballet class in the untarnished morning
to have had a mother at all?
did she even know what it meant to be a true and devout
mother
or did she deal in confusion and fear and silent conferences
with god
praying her daughter would suffer as she had-
with that same pain-bred
cruelty lining her lips?
do you ever wonder
if jesus cried on the cross?
not for himself or his father
but for the giving blood of his mother
spilling down the crown of his skull for a second time
shielding his eyes for the first
warming him in that glittering ruby blanket for the last
and even if he didn't feel it
it was there
she was always there
she always will be there
in her recurring easter
until the fruit the earth can give is only rot.

i can fight this
i can fight it
ability has never truly been that wicked contest
but strength of the soul
hardness of the heart
yielding the gentleness embedded within
the soft medicinal pink
i am not ready to give up my pride in purity-
my security in silky tones-
for the sake of winning a battle i did not begin
i strive to retain that which makes me weaker
i strive to lose all wars and fight with pale hands
so i may be delicate and barely outlined
only a whisper of a woman
i have violently peeled away the desperation in those eyes
shed the niceness
for kindness

it knew her better than she knew herself
for it had seen and scanned into memory every single dirty,
crowded,
shame-burst
part of her lush consciousness
so maximalist in her emotions
it had made that black dust rot horror into a childhood friend
the way it was
recognizable through breath alone
it was in the darkest corner
kicking the dust into the air and watching it settle
only ever having one question

her bones could crumple
dissolve into the disgusting dorm room carpet until she could
be vacuumed and discarded and given to the earth to be free
crushing
million ton sadness by brand
hand still over her monstrous heart as if in solemn respect
for the national anthem
shut up
shut up
shut up

a wretched moment between us
stretched between tip and tongue of three
maybe four months
a ruinous evil
that you let pour your own greedy migraine in my eyes
took it as a task
on a game show
a momentary risk for a desperate grab for a ridiculous prize
for the girl who rode her bike past you that one time
and cried for the sake of crying another
but all the daughter in me really truly wanted
was to hold a hand and be shepherded
did it really have to be so cruel?
it cost me everything before i had even
been alive long enough
to understand what my everything should be worth

oh, the waste!
oh, the waste!
of a heart
of a life
of a pretty face
to be in such a lamented state-
but oh,
the potential!
once the heart is an ugly and fingerprinted legend
is it not time to discard?
and oh,
dear
sweet
god
the wasteland
and oh! the wasteland
how the ground there absolutely breathes and sinks and soaks
itself up for you
covered in blood and teeth
unfinished letters and unfinished dinners
but you will be finished
and done
and so
oh!
how darling it is
that to the waste you go.

i could have been a mother
if not for the lightning strike that broke my heart and tunneled
my vision
from the world around mine body
to the world inside
to wet blood unyielding red between my toes
never ceased, i bleed still
but i killed my body
it killed me in return
and all but black mourning felt immature, girlish, weak
it was a mature pain
a maternal longing
a wild and ferocious roar of wind that nobody could yet hear
for i absorbed it in my bitten cheeks still
bruised and broken and skinny and angry and so hurt
so hurt
worth far less by weight with water than an ambulance ride
twenty-two thousand dollars.
one thousand cotton bolls for every year i have yet planted
here
for her
for her
for her
for her
for her

this skin begs to be caressed by the air of a place i
cannot
cannot
cannot
return to
it pulls and reaches away from me in waves
crashing with the unbridled rage of a displaced child
never receipted nor returned
never unpackaged or undressed
never to rest in that airy sweetness
for some internal divine arrangement sworn in blood
far out of her tiny hands' reach
and too too close
for their comfort

in trying to keep the devil's lick-ed fingers out of my house
away from my love
i immortalized myself only within optional pages and spaces
and now the devil is wick-ed in my brain and my heart flames
ferocious
thaws my frozen bones and i cannot pen it out
that heat, so tremendous
there is no escaping myself this time

man who knows me
must stop immediately
there is none true knowledge left of me
to be found in as unsympathetic a soul as his
there is no place warm to lay my head
as bruised and fresh surged
still bleeding

man who knows me is not able to keep
those thoughts at bay of what he might do if i were to
touch another
lay eyes on another
they consume him
consume me through his eyes
strengthen his grip and his unwashed fingers pulling
my ribbon too tight until it falls to the ground and i am
simply
unable
to become a pretty girl again

man who will always treat me
like a traitorous witch who has stolen something so sacred
from him
though i fly his flag as a guard
with such honor and pride
such tradition
never like a friend he could offer just any darling little favor
to
could that not be the source of all my unrest
in my fragile little bird's lifespan?

how to become this
amazing discount all women are
and then i said
can you believe you'll never believe this
are you paying attention to the state of
sex
sex
sex
and i wouldn't say it if it weren't true believe me
believe me
believe me
fifty five percent off of my
nudes linked now
watch me
watch me
watch me
tell me i look pretty
do i look my age
do i look younger
do i look freshly birthed from my wicked mother's wretched
womb do i look
just spilled from creation
my trade secret to sparkle
less than a cup of coffee
less than
less
read my watch my listen to my song song song words look at
me look at me look at me why will you not look at me why
will you not listen
can't you hear my voice in this clamorous din?
isn't it sharp enough
special enough

skin too wrinkled too clear transparent
she must be mean to be so pretty
she must devour the hearts of every man who dares love her
the women the mother,
devoured the mother
her mother
her mother
was once a little girl too
are you listening-

maybe if i could put all my transgressions into smaller words
to float more comfortable in the digital canon
though i am temporary
though i am
but temporarily
my eyes voice smile laugh thoughts every waking thought
every
miniscule opinion
every single damned breath
i want to live forever and i want
to never cease in wanting something more
something bigger than everything that will ever exist
in this gray grass landscape

something could be nurtured now, here, in this body
for the first time in years it could harvest
but all it wanted was not what i imagined
rather, two steps outside
something so large it could never be bridled or broken
never would its hands hold a child in its own image
no karmic being cared to measure the yearning
cared to watch the wanting
cared to reward the suffering

the lace in my bonnet becomes as i
wearied and yellowed and loosened with time
though it may stiffen, to maintain its lines
it falters in heat
in humidity
it cries

but i
though not for want
am stronger than my weave
i do not buckle or break in that fierce southern heat
and the way i am made is not to deceive
not to promise a girlish demeanor
not to elude the meanness of my sisters
but to bare my teeth
when offered your finger

to glisten and gleam only when dirty
and dull underneath a coarse hand with polish
to shimmer and shine in the darkest of nights
and forgive all so that i may become how i wished to inherit
sweet and supple and kind

although the mirror of time may offer some reprieve, i
do not gladly admire myself for who i was
but slap my own wrist for whom i have become
there were no fiercer flames than those i was born to
and i will return to that familiar burn when all is done
but i will wait
until the sun has scorched my image onto every
facet of stone in the appalachian mountains
until nobody can forget what they ignored
tried to veil and disguise, with that pretty white
lace that fell before me
withered
and died.

you slaughtered my devastation
solemn sister sadness
there will be no forgiveness for that
you awful, simple creature
for how empty it has made me-
a woman shaped in such a kiln only to hold
sorrow and anger-
when happiness is hardly half the weight

there had been such friendship there
and no lover will ever hold me
that way again
no god could ever answer my prayers
yet, even to listen
as mine own duplicate image did
my horrid, beautiful thing
laid to rest.

she deserved the same chance as i
but you would not understand it
the inherent pride in pain, in bearing it like a whinging infant
against your breast
you would not know what it means
to nurture something that pains you,
and love it all the same

the creekbed billows naked
the trees bend to kiss
they feel you here
pray to only you
breathe and sway to soothe you
so endeared to you
i am so like them
in this way
with my willow-back spine
and my permanent sway.

what a devastating series
to slice the smallest cuts into every stitched-up panel
advertised to be so breathable
but the weight of weightlessness bowed the bone
transformative
and the endeavors of the emotionless broke the spirit
reformative
the capturing presence caught sand and caging hands
and drew nothing but nausea and memory loss
with an expired fence contract of six years
not a moment too soon
destructive

she grows impatient now
fingernails that peel my skin as an apple
wet and shining pale
half-moon scattered red
she grows much hungrier now
restless
air has not satisfied her, nor the lack of it
no amount of time asphyxiated could cure this
no matter how much liquid fills the lungs
nothing could give her solace, reprieve
forgiveness from being so cruelly chained in
the back of my mind
that mean girl i
try i
pretend i
have never known

nobody ever questioned
the state of my emptied pockets
in regards to
the state of my emptied mind
but i think they could not even begin to bear it
to be complicit in my dissolution,
to have prayers answered without my knowledge
to cage me in a safety much like a hospital bed-
not unlike the ones i remember-
with the bars along the sides in case i
leaked my sadness into the hallway and
poisoned the kindness of the woman who
held me down and took my shaking signatures
and what am i to do if not
kill
myself?
what is left in this
stupid
taskless
space of
nothing
so i play my romance records on
and on
and become
defiant and damned in the
repetitive nature that is my
young adulthood in all of its
cursed feminine urges
to yearn and look pretty while yearning
spin and spin and spin
in a dress with a history
until absolute in my broken nature

vomit stomach acid
dizzy from the lack of true sustenance in my
heart soul stomach
and ungracefully close my
sandpaper eyes
so they can rest
while my body is alight
sleepy and starved
but never could i dare
to remain stationary in my personality
for fear of remaining stationed
in a piece of time
that is not to be looked at any longer
every motion is a eulogy
sweet dedication
the world was so beautiful
when i became devoured by my pain
so tranquil colored bright when i was a dark cloud
where now the sun cannot rise to meet me
in my technicolor exterior
what a metamorphosis-
a brand new kind of plague
swept through all you know
but at least you were allowed to know it

a darling in venus
perching on a shoulder with the sharpest tongue
possessed her hair to grow a preferable length
wrapped its number-ribbons 'round her waist
in a dizzying dance seeking nausea, a splint, a cast

but venus grew
like a young vine,
much too eager to play with the weeds and the trees
that darling shadowed her roots-
pruned and plucked her and suck-ed the marrow juice from
her little vine-stems

until venus,
even in her sunshine glory
curled up towards the moon and looked back
at her little darling shadow-how it did reach towards her
always
peeled one of her own leaves back and bled a scream out that
shook the entire earth

must i trigger motherhood in you to feel simply loved,
or will my greatest accomplishment be in my end-time?
what an intolerable misery to be born with; what a vicious
port-stain, my inability to identify my own source in you.

and no matter how the darling did kiss and cradle that sweet
naked vine there, sorrowful and sweetened and sorry-ing the
stars away
venus had gone to be with her true moon-mother
and never could return.

how could you
lift your hand that way
as though i was invincible
and you were a victim?
and then,
to ask for a truce
with a billowing white flag
smeared with my own blood?
i would pick all the paint off of my walls
and swallow it
before i would even try to
understand your mind
any empathetic simulation does forever
erase who i was there
satisfies nothing

i don't feel that human hunger anymore
i don't feel the time pass
i don't feel the sun settle on my skin
does it burn?
does it hurt?
am i losing something?
am i doing it right?
you wouldn't like it if you could hear the echoes inside my
esophagus
it would sound so raw, like that night
i cried so hard i vomited into your carpet
and felt my teeth decay in real time as your eyes burned
straight through my nervous system
still, i couldn't stop
and i thought, maybe an angel did this to me
maybe this is a test from god
maybe somebody sent a prayer into the blood of the wretched
world for my sake
and i really was protected
but no invisible hand did pluck me
from my invisible pains
and my hysteria was up to my eyelashes as it enveloped me
but i still lived
despite everything
so now only pain is my legacy

i think about them every day
the darling girls of my youngest years
who lived next to me
played in my backyard
with the foxes and the flower petals
that always lined
the ditch behind
who rode the bus with me
who fought the boys who
held me down to kiss me and pull my hair
who stole the laughs out of his mouth when it was about me
and
hid them in their tightest braids
kept me near their hearts when their hearts were changing
faster than even the phases of the moon could keep up with
i think about them every time i am awake before dawn
in the way someone who holds a lukewarm mug
as if it could still burn would
my stillborn pieces of girlhood arranged as a puzzle
on the floor of every bathroom i have ever cried in
i wonder if they think about me too
emily or amanda or sara or nancy or sam
i wonder if their lives are as beautiful as i had foreseen
when a smaller skin fitted my bones

he looks at me like a gorgeous, unbroken piece
of delicate porcelain in this light
he looks at me like i was never ugly in high school
like i was never propositioned for threesomes
like i am still a chosen virgin at my own will
like i still possess myself and myself alone
like i was never a sore subject on anybody's unbitten tongue
he looks at me like i am not biodegradable-
like i am a shimmering piece of priceless forever plastic
like i do not taste flesh in my dreams
and i suppose there had been a time where i questioned why
it was so easy for him
when before
it felt, if i remember correctly,
like i had volunteered to be at war
knowing i would never have been drafted
and i suppose i could have asked the bigger men in my life
why they felt so small
but i was busy spinning
in a secret picnic of sunlight and
naturally-sweetened sorrows
while he looked at me, and only me, and always me
and i looked at him
and only him
and always him

why didn't you bear me in such a way? i ask the tree
from my spot on the earthen floor
it hears me, but does not answer
it grows already new fruit, more of me
but younger
and i am already a day old
i rot at her feet and sink into my age as it becomes me and i
become it and all i am is previously established and not to be
changed
she will absorb me
all i have left to become is forgotten
but i fear i have even become too old to imagine that, though
i still lie within her sight
so i cannot help but cry, sour apple tears
any stranger could love me at first bite
any passerby could imagine me plated beside their dominant
hand on a
painlessly flavorless cloudy tuesday afternoon
but she thinks she already did those things when i was but a
seed of myself
and the bright, new apple glowing red in her eyes, perched
within her bough lying closest to her heart
reflects any memory of me into some outside place
for it is not my turn to be held
and the time to sleep in a mother's arms is long gone
now i only sleep at her sacrificial feet
and fertilize her anger
with nightly melodious prayers for a renewal
for forgiveness

eleven years ago
i formed my body to the will of a man
i had thought was my age
but was twelve years older
in a desperate aching plea as i
clung to him clinging to me
throughout the nights of my ripe youth
not even grown
i longed to be fawned over
though i was still a fawn myself
to be unsupervised in my wild heart
and how it beat in an off-putting way
now i hate it
where is the romance without
desperate pleas for tiny hands to pluck from a
self-sustained panic of damnation
where is the love without the threat of suicide-
for if there is no violence to be saved from,
how do i know he could have saved me at all?

that cruel mother
that unyielding thorn
that insufferable little girl
young woman
full of remorse
raised in me
my only legacy as a woman
is the pain wrought on all before me
to scorch the earth long after
with the bleeding rage of a daughter

there is a body, lying there
in a hole at my feet
i have this dream once a week
some maroon smoke of a force
with a voice
tells me to grab it
and i, for some godforsaken reason
place a permanent curve in my spine with the weight of the
lifelessness
grabbed by the hair
i can still feel the weight in the tensile fragility of that
delicate scalp in my hand
i drag the body behind me, all the time wondering why it is
naked
but braided
with bows
and it has tattoos, just alike to my own body
and the eyes are my color blue
incredulous
nauseated
that in my life,
i feel so heavy in my sadness and rage and unspoken hurt
while in death,
i weigh nothing at all

i know now
i will lose everything against my will
and pick pieces of it out from under
my fingernails
there will never be peace
i know now that
fighting for quiet
will only ever make more noise
and hiding is the way of
the adult responsibility

she was so heartbreaking to watch
"i think it is okay now"
was all she would say
but she cried when she sat
on that side of the car
and studied her hands
at every dining table
she had filled that apartment
with every noise she could make
but she had been prematurely
mourned
as she drowned in some
spectacular glittering dream
some atomic fantasy
where love was the meaning of life
and she was made of love
but it hadn't been enough
not to save her
and all she would say when asked about it
by starving artists who yearned for
secondhand torture was
"i think it is okay now"

somebody will hate all this
someone will think it to be too repetitive
too melodramatic
too verbose in descriptions of what should be
in the mind of a man who has never been loved by a man
a simple pain
but it was never simple
and it ate me alive with so much feeling it radiated
if i even could plainly talk about what happened
i wouldn't
i brought them all my heart as a child
with the prettiest weed
plucked from a farmhouse
in oklahoma once did
in a way that primed me for staggering pain
until all i was
and all i bled
was silly and useless and wretched

the clinical nature of a sterile mouth
fresh-birthed spoiled
not yet opened
not yet consuming
only a perfect hole for a delicate emptiness
and such tiny hands so soft and sateen
the littlest doll to be unboxed
but they lit a candle for it and let it remain unnamed
buried it beneath a tree in a wild animal refuge
so the devastation could not run so
ruinous and wild
but it was in vain
for an unnamed child
has
every
name
and an unborn being
carries
every
face
and endless amounts of a soul
float wild and thick
like dead skin in the tap water
it was an idiotic choice
to attempt to limit the undescribed ghost's ability to
haunt
and now nothing can be told
for there was never anything to say
that could explain it without it
tearing the stitches
and nobody ever wanted to peer into
the depths of an

ever-infected gut wound
the solemn six-month chill
that soaked every fire ever lit there
in an attempt to
cauterize
and no amount of sleep could dull the dream
 unfulfilled for an eternity ever-outlasting
everyone that spoke of it into an
empathetic glass of red wine
amongst a club of
dry-mouthed
pornographically voyeuristic
emotional
vultures
i turned twenty-one somewhere in those six weeks
relinquished my birthday to the grip of an
anniversary
and shed the memory of a lullaby in the dark
easier digestion than a fingernail

the demon had haunted her since she was thirteen
marked her differently
marked her disturbed
a sexual deviant
burned alive at the stake of her own
diseased moral clause
but when she recognized it in him
a darling stranger
and turned to run
he grabbed her by the hair
poured liquor that stung like nostalgia into her eyes
smiled with all of his teeth
and she saw her soul reflected
in the back of his throat
as he said
she knew him already

he wrote about me
a recreationally hideous comedy
for fun
i never read it
too busy furiously emptying my mind
it had been at the doctor's behest
to cleanse me of the hysteria
in the end
they deemed me a permanent mark on somebody else's
perfect record
and there was absolutely nothing left that was my own
not even my insanity knew me
not like it knew him

would they attempt to rehabilitate with chains
if it came out again
would they say they had always known
moribund things untold
and sit with woven limbs in that same deranged
acrimonious amphitheater
tuck their hair behind their ears
widen their deserted eyes to the brim
in a feeble parody of sympathy
smiling only to carry
as a badge
the remnants of pride between their teeth
a pack of dogs with a mediocre bounty
more or less a fine-tuned chorus with the way they could
perfectly harmonize their
aching tongues in cruel misunderstanding
an animal mimicry of their mothers

the memory was dream-like
how three months could turn so sour
those minds turned quicker than a glance
when the competition marathoner did pause

the relentless agony became a macrocosm
how to absorb such power
proper breath a rarity in a chemically unstable atmosphere
norepinephrine a permanent replacement
draft restoration of a victorian disposition in a swift divorce

a word was used but not understood
somehow a prophecy, a premonition the first of its kind
a departed heart withering in a lime-scaled bathtub
a stubborn death rattle
twenty-five hours of weak survival
not a chance to change divine will

you were the wind that rang the church bell
the bat in my attic
the shards of glass where an image of me once had stood and
posed
so delicately, to impress you
my sweetest unrelenting judge
a key player in the roleplay that fed my heart
processed affection until it was clogged and gasping
as my tired body finally gave out in the shower
i truly did not survive
hot april in solitary confinement
scolded for trusting you by every matron that turned my bed
you were a little girl's death omen
as something carbon was unwillingly born
on the eve of my passing

infatuation enkindled beneath my feet like a wildfire
there was no chance of any realistic escape
he could have swallowed me entirely
but the way he held me on the pyre
it reignited a long-lost faith
smelled of mine own flesh
kissed me on the collar
offered me peace
gave me death
stole any disturbance from my home
and the decrepit disappeared
with every inch closed between us
i became closer to understanding god

when i walk
i walk alongside mine own image
staring at herself in the shop windows
cursing with rage when the foggy distortion meets her toes
and she watches me so intently
studying me
she did not graduate college
i am all she knows

she wants to know what i look like
in a way that feels inhumane
she hungers for angles i have never seen
i walk alongside myself
but she is different
she is not entirely me

she cannot be me
for i want far too badly to become her

my mother says often
if the devil cannot reach you
he will send a big chocolate cake
and if he can reach you
you must be thin enough to bleed between the spaces in his
fingers
or you will not be saved

but i fear the devil reached me
caught me ensnared in some
ratchet-strapped barbed-wire wrapped cage
and now i am handcuffed by pointer finger and pinky finger

67

there is a curious bird
it watches through every window
every pane of glass exists within the refraction of its gaze
i clutch the crucifix lasso-tied 'round my sore throat
i pray for god to save me
it tells me to save myself
he knows not what i need saving from
he knows not
for
if i could never be god
there is no way he could have ever been me
that bird screeches at me
resounding screams in both ears
they sound like mine as a little girl
i pray to be his perfect girl
pretty and clean and well-rounded
but the devastation he entrusted me with
is a plague, a disease, incurable, wasting
and his reasoning seems unfounded
he is simply another father figure
claiming your body is not
bloating
stretching to carry
the weight of his many sins

She is that pure wildflower-thing
all the mirrors in
the ballet studio
the gym
the airport
the mall even the
windows they would break themselves to bend to
Her in a more flattering reflection
and it must've been the roll of the specific syllables
off the tongues of the masses that made Her so

She probably doesn't even bleed
so perfectly insulated,
a stuffed doll full of rice and fiberglass and crisp cotton and
white swan feather
could it be that Her skin is laced with cocaine?
could it be that when She smiles
She has one extra tooth that glitters pure white-
that fills a hole no human born prior even imagined they had?
has She somehow escaped the simulacrum and become that
thing
become the one-to-be-imitated?
how was She built
with god's third hand

and will i ever feel that hand touch me or
am i forced to touch myself forever?

it was reckless of me to live without warrant
i know that now, and in a way i always have
but,
as the punches roll in,
one after another and another

another
                    another
another
there is something
a comfort
i begin to find
in the taste of your blood braided with mine

two wretched creature-things
hold the darkness like a blanket
a delicate and glassy duvet

two beaten bodies
fall over and over
again down that devoured quarry-side
there is no skin left to scrape and no cuticle to chew but
nothing to chew for

four tired hands
face their wounds toward god

a golden offer still stands to become a curse yet
but battling your phobias and fears has become
my natural obsession
knighted by tears from those much stronger than i
with my hands
i could cleanse you
with my eyes
i could understand that which you
are afraid to be naked for
not fix you
just love you

something is there
in all my nights
something is with me
it is so small in that cracked door-light strip
but it is definitely there

something betrays me

it cannot help but be heard
loud and squealing and crying at me
it cannot help anything at all
i stole its home
i stole its everything
something is definitely there

something betrays me

i swallowed all my air and emptiness
became the blackest hole
sucked it all up and shit it all out
and ruined everything

i became horrific and tragic and angry and then peace
invaded me
but horror was stuck on my fingers and hands and naked toes
when my thumb was suckled for comfort and joy after thus
long
all those years and months and minutes and minutes
horror was stuck in its mouth once more
i learned it from somewhere
whispers of the devil
i learned it from somewhere

silence of the god
i learned it from somewhere
whispers of the devil
cries of the lamb
something is there

something betrays me

i am only a mirror of mine previously precious image now
a devious and devilish
heart-breaking
gut-wrenching
scene-starting
fight-finishing
blood-letting
tear jerking soot cloud
i am only a mirror
something is still there

something has betrayed me

there is a light
i feel i feel it
there is a light
i see myself seeing it
drawing closer to me now
with silver beckoning hand
drawing me closer now
drawing me
as someone i have never been before
some truth in death
to see it does change you eternally
i solemnly sit
i allow the curtains to be only
half-closed
i await a surely excruciating end

awareness of the self is
what keeps me still in my bed
paralyzed by the feeling
i possess a knowledge
not meant for me
my house has become just a house
but my body has become a cage
and my fingers shake and crackle
no longer does blind confidence
propel my motions
i see everything
i see everything
i see everything

the wild heart that ensnares the mind
does screech and scream
for some beckoning finger that cannot be seen
and my body is not my body
and my home is not my home
my blood only exists in sound alone
and the drip
   drip
drip
reminds my person of what frail fragility
possesses a creature like me
crawling and crying in a shadow
unbeknownst to others
all too aware of myself

how much and little
what variety of numbers can be contained
by such a sickly body
what variety of numbers can be restrained
by such a sickening mind

unable to be laid out with fingers or lips
all that can be said is
the raw meat has been cut cleanly
thin and rare
and i am in pain

imagine a black lake
the sand is black
the water is black
the sky is dusky gray
and you are always tired

your mother calls you down for dinner and you scream at her
she doesn't know why you feel the way you feel
and you are torn between slipping through the sand and
crawling away from the water-you want to tell her
she wouldn't understand.

she would
she knows
but she doesn't know it like you do.
that's what the men say
when they talk about how small your body is
or how pretty you are
you're so smart for your age.

and of course, they're right.

two of your best friends are buried before you ever meet them
one of cancer
one of something equally treacherous, equally difficult to
treat
you dream of them,
you think of that scene from that library book you dropped in
the bathtub
where her body is hanging from the ceiling.
it calms you

the same way that temporary pains and momentary losses
thrill you
and you never stop
never wondering who you are - you know who
and then, three more are dead
and you have no funerals to attend.

five more fake their deaths for your attention.
two more send you pictures of their wrists slashed before
being hospitalized.
one of those two still posts, but you don't talk.
they've outgrown that sort of intimacy
you've outgrown that sort of psychological torture.

you are the one who stares at the asses of every girl walking
in front of you in the hallways at school
measuring in your head
how many inches between their thighs
how many calories in an apple
your best friend asks you
of course, you know.
you're doing so well.
you still do that now, at twenty-three.
you still measure your body with your fingers.
a harbinger of death
a priestess of decaying flesh
your breath still stinks
your teeth turn to grit between themselves

a stranger online has photos of you
her name was kaylee

she was your age
his name is unbeknownst to you
you hide your ipod in a closet
stare at yourself in the mirror and cry
and help your mother unload the groceries
wondering if people really eat all that
knowing you will succumb to it soon
you wonder if what he said was true
about having your best interests at heart
you leave the group chat that is
dedicated to helping each other lose weight
yet another friend group lost because of you
you plot an escape
you plot an escape
you plot an escape
but he never does it
your body never graces the internet
now, you understand why
now, you understand a lot of things

even in the description of torture there is a twinkle of
romance
to be able to spell out the suffering in words makes it so
beautiful, so rare
but it is not rare
it is being a teenage girl
and it is not darling or interesting
it stinks and rots and claims you
and you become mean and angry and cruel
as it is mean and angry and cruel
it is not gorgeous

it is not beautiful to be
constantly consumed with being beautiful
it is not beautiful to be
constantly consumed with being beautiful
it is not beautiful to be
constantly consumed-

i need it!
because need is fiercer in flame than want
want is expunged
need is inspired
born to vine-net the cardiovascular and become the spine
need becomes excruciating
need becomes everything!

no memory remains of a birthcoming
a homecoming
there is only the plight of one who attaches herself to
something attainable
in the hopes of forgetting that which is fantastical
just to be left dissatisfied
but i still yearn in the crook of that withered antler-shed
suckling the blood from the wallpaper wrapped
all there is to know is wanting

i want it so badly!
it burns me;
i need it so ferociously!
it kills me.

please
on my hands
please
on my knees
please
on my tongue
please
in the toilet bowl
please
underneath my fingernails

do you exist only to suffocate yourself in the presence
of those who have previously felt suffocated by yours?

please
says the pulpit
hands stretched high
please
cries the pews
knees bloody buckled on the
velvet-tacked wood

do i exist only to satisfy some sick experimental need
in some impossible god physician?

down there'n by that honeysuckle bush
where he suckl'd my life away
my little mountain love is buried
a gift on a bed of bobbin lace
oh, say he was so loved
his mama wept as the fair madonna
two feathers in her hair
knees above the head
of her sacr'ficed lamb boy
but beneath the seep
of his sin-stained sleep
lies that crook'd garden sickle
and beneath the layers
of my breezy mourning white
burns a forget-me-not scarred
so when i go yond'r to make
my tearful confessions
i will say how the blood blew the wind softer
and grow'd the trees greener
and opened my eyes wider
and i sure am gladdened
to have killed my little mountain love
lest he kill me first

i set myself on the bed
willed it all to take me
breathing heavily
always so unsteady in my demeanor
carrying my body far below my weight
in a solemn prayer
when hope for redemption goes
half-swallowed in that solitary night
the question of continuation becomes
unbearably unbearable
unmanageable, unmanageable

a shot with a rubber bullet still weaves
a bloody flight
when i am comprised of something
far softer than flesh
far above a fox-hunt

long may your blood serve the waters
of your family sightline
what a heavy truth
what an asphyxiating velvet curtain draped
desperately tossed as a fly-net
over all that was
dirty hands and feet scrambling to become
some gentle giant in your innocently glimmering eyes
that young babe only whines in pleads and prayers
a pale beckoning fingernail on a string becomes
the entire world

long may the sterility of your absence serve the mind
a reminder of how delicately
infancy does fall

trimmings of the sex have seemed to me
the best way to eliminate the weight
ten pounds of wretched breast
fifteen of scarred uterine
a rotted pear-womb
sexless and thin
silent and pacified by
the appeal of the proximity
to being a real woman

you know,
it is sickening
to sleep somehow whilst knowing
reality exists in the relaxed space
between my numbed fingers
even as i clutch my weeping chest
and wring it into words of nonsense
and then walk away from this
cloudy puddle i have become
the puddle remains
i remain
it all is stilled even without my
shivering gaze
my fearful eyes so scared of witnessing
the time finishes its task with or without
my being present
the breath comes even when i
do not will it to come
the sun burns and blisters my skin
even while i am not there to feel it
my skin feels it
my skin and i
my skin feels it still

don't trust the apple
that never has been bit
chewed and swallowed

it doesn't know how it feels
to have your decay
displayed in such a way

it doesn't know the sting of
fresh air on a
gaping wound
but it wants to

so disgusting
that sickening overestimation
of the reaches
of the wingspan
of an empathetic angel

what happened to us?

what do you mean, us?

control is coated in slick
and impossible for me to find
so thrilling
the conversations between mind and self and heart and
womanhood
how they leave me bruised
agape and gasping
parallel universes birthed within
the circumference of my
infant skull
the cause of that
constant pressure on
my damned head
the infernal device that hardens
my voice and
sharpens
my nerves
to spears
with no control still
and slippery hands
a thieving failure in the night
a ribboned piece of skin flapping in the wind
dry and hinged so uncomfortably

that feeling
that exists in the cessation of feeling
that most dangerous of tide pools
in my heavy eyelids, i find apathy
but in apathy, i recover my bruised melancholia
her weepings seem to soothe
a flood current is approaching
and i am drown-ed
my head held woman-less in her lap
my hair curling in yellow ribbons
'round her snick-ed and sliced-up skin

you leave such a trembling in your wake
o' dearest darling
you leave such a wistful wanting
o' stranger there
my imagination explodes upon itself
o' pressure fair
love is so dry and cruel to its lusting buzzard
you are my annihilation and my dehydration

o' the drugs
how they trudge
but my heart is wined by you
and the graze of a canine renders me
but a woman
o' smallest hare
a prey animal gnawing
at mine thin limbs
o' danger true
desperate to remove
the trapping glue

faces mean nothing to my soul
when they all appear to have snake-ish tendrils of finger
protruding from mousy eyes
and all i feel is a lack of you
but while you were hinged at the waist over a sparkling pool
leeching love from your own reflection
i was bent at all joints
arthritic in my proselytizing
hands tin and outstretched and echoing empty

when i sank my indulgent fangs into the love left there
it burned my throat and singed my skin
blistered and bubbled and boiled
laced with guilt
as all love seems to be, these days as i find
myself feeling a personal jailer for loving you
this infinite tether to still you against my restless soul
my wither-beating heart
and when i bake you bread
you claw through the smoke and swallow a burning and tell
me
it tastes delicious
there, right there
that is the guilt of turning you
into a liar by loving you
turning you into a caged predator by baring my abdomen
and crying at you to never bite me as the saliva
foams at the hinges of your lips

the babe awoke at noon with the smoky call
of a stilled and suffocating sun
she rose above the mist
shocking to have again endured the
night-stalking damage of her kin
something postural
psy cho so ma tic

she expected pain with the rising
found none
stretched her twiggy limb-things far back
and wide against the will of her
stiffer spine
found pain again
but admonished was she
for seeking comforts

some organ plucked from her body had potentially
carried that pain with it across that creek that
ribbon-laced the land
traced the hand
to feed it back into a wet and sleeping mouth
it had been lodged in a soundless mud to be
retrieved, returned to the pulp of her heart
a gift, a gift, a gift

the rotted tooth of regret peels itself
from bloodied lip and frayed gum and crackling jaw
to sink into your wrists
you cannot go outside
it snaps as it breaks through scar tissue
you cannot go outside
your veins burst and shout in a
violent poppy-red as fourth of july fireworks
against the wall you cannot
you cannot go outside
when your mother calls you cannot go
outside
you are not in the pictures
you are not on the walls
you are not in the memories
you do not exist at all

some invisible force has pulled me back with a father's hands
but here i stand, still
at the edge of something more fatherly
it holds me

it is a mature presence
it won't allow me to carry it on my back, yet
it kisses me as a gun
tickling the back of my throat

i do not yet know what i am to know about knowing
do not know that every ten paces towards a bulb does
illuminate my backside
my frontside shadowed

i do not know i cannot turn around
i still think that backwards plain is mine and mine alone and
sculpted by
the father, the father
my forward face still shines so wet and innocent

yet, the happiness leaks through every pore
the mother-dirt eats it all
and i still mourn oh, i still cry to being born properly, wisely
with the weight of the muscle required to carry itself

my father, my mother
my atrophied brain wilted

she taps the lily-of-thine-valley against her cheek until it
becomes
itching and gnawing
until the sensation is isolating in its irritation
and she must move along her body
there is no choice,
only compulsion in all its faces

it cannot be rewritten
those years do not scream to be
squeezed out of the stomach
nor vomited from the sponge
dripped dry over an aching tongue
so there is mourning
and restless crying
and it is factual
but not comfortable
the new skin is taught by the wrinkle of the old
it all forms as once was,
as has been as it has
to be forevermore

the anatomy of a pedestal
truly lies in the foundation
that is how the scholars suggest it
the strength in the piece to indicate
the ways in which it can be used

the anatomy of a pedestal is
not widely known
the physiology seems definition enough
to assume true knowledge of the form
complexity, a waste of thinking

the anatomy of a pedestal
similar to that of a step-ladder with no steps
no gradation
to be straddled and breathed over and
prop and push and extend and enlighten
quietly

my spine seems but a stage,
but a stage, these days

the writing heals you
the words bleed straight from your palms and it feels
it feels like purification, but
it leeches all life from your lips
and you can never read it again
not if you value your heart's gentle nature
and wish to forget the self that bled you dry

love found me gentle-eyed and waiting
deep in a chasm of grief and decay
and it made me a character of strength
i found a mother in love
and left the daughters of my past buried
with floral arrangements and brass name-plates
and when i felt as an animal with dirt beneath my
tired claws and shattered nails, love passed me the shovel
with which to dig my final resting place

twenty-three makes each year a bruise
for every heart that overtook my own
the palpitation rumbling builds in exponential success
like heavy, black boot stumbling upside steel step
every motion of my body has become an act of prayer
every bend of my knee reminiscent of when i begged
even the joy feels a
delicate foam amidst a
swirling wave
fragility is everywhere
and i am scared to breathe heavier
than a dandelion-breath
scared to shake away the minutia that has
caused me comfort
as i ring my twenty-fourth bell

i am at my most evil as the sun teases from behind
the sturdy city skyline
when my makeup feels slick on my face
and my stomach feels bile-heavy and
the anxiety of facing a new day the same person
crushes me into the carpet
why must the done remain done?
when the weight of my sins presses me against the
coldest surface and leaves me pinned against a cross
of mine own design- why is rebirth not an option for
the girls with heavy childhoods and runaway minds?
i know it kills you to see it all disappear before your
tender gaze, i know it must be so difficult to watch
as the fountain-pen prickled skin peels and flutters to the
floor

a series of tubes and bubbling liquids a fleshy feeding trough
carved into a lip-shape at the reproductive organs
a blessing upon the earth, and earth as its blessing
an object of disgust in the aftershocks of enjoyment
but never alive never alive never alive an incubator
a tool, curved to fit warm and velveteen in the skin-tearing
calloused grip of those who would wield with teeth curved as
a rabbit and blood-sap drawn as a tree

a poorly drawn science lesson begs an important question that
will go endless in ridicule and grief and the mocking cries of
cackling peers that do not understand the question of safety is

as a sandbag perched not so delicate upon
such fragile shoulder, still developing collar-bone
a woman's skeleton is curved in painful ways from the
earliest age to account for those who may hope to find solace
within it and sit lazily in the conversation pit of her throat-
vacuumed stomach and pornographically arched spine

when the women clothe themselves in the early afternoons
with ribbons and laces and adorn their private bodies with
artifacts of childhood and you question why why why would
you wish to be a child again why would you crave stupidity
you beg of the creature that has never known the profound
solace of the masculine art of not knowing
but there is no again
there never was a child within her
for a woman is formed as a woman the second she escapes
the slippery womb of her mother and becomes no longer a
parasite but a most precious and virginal host presented

as an offering for those who may beg of her
years before her time
years before she even bleeds for herself,
the chances of her bleeding for someone else are a true and
black devastation
as all women did before her,
as all women will again

the thundering roar of young adulthood is dying, now
there is just a long and straight and tireless wind
sweeping over the dry brush of the texan plains
that strings and strands my hair and whips and burns my skin
i don't think i like myself
my turbulent poetry and hideous artwork that i slip
between my skin as small blades and hope to claw out
someday when the screaming has ceased
my teeth yellowed from years of vomiting
longer, still, of not bothering to care for them at all
my hair like hay as it brushes the dry skin of my back,
never soft or smooth or shiny like the pretty girls
my inability to find joy in the simple acts of living
without daydreaming a setting in which the
mundane becomes celebrity and i am beloved
by those who despise me and i can find solace
in the arms of strangers
because there are no strangers
when everyone knows you
i just wanted to be proud
i just wanted to be proud
i just wanted to be proud
i just wanted all of those people
who found fault in me
to someday see that inside,
a hot star was cooling and
bubbling off
i wanted them to find pride in knowing me
instead i found hatred and disdain
from everyone
forever

i think death is
all of the selves i have had
sleeping gentle in the same bed
as the rain pours against
sheer-curtained windows
and the sun illuminates
precious artifacts of living

i have been thinking, much to my disadvantage
between swells and breaks and shakes
and cries of wanting to go home
-but home is a
mental hospital and i am a bleeding tomato beneath its
textured non-slip sole-
that i will never feel the way i was starting to
not ever again, not with you
everything has changed
in just that wrong way, and i am leaking
leaking and leaking
this state is horribly empty without you in it
and i am horribly empty to not smell you in the breeze-
memory
all is alone always alone always crying alone, here
grief is productive, i was told, i was told

i have not formed my own opinion of it save for how it
t r u d g e s on layered thick as tar that never heals
some natural rage that justly refuses cooling
sticks and stains like i dragged my hem through wet cement

grief cannot braid my hair
grief cannot fill my palm
grief cannot feed my body and drag it to the bathroom
grief despises the cyclical waste of living
so it seems to be useless
it can only pin me down
infect me with sickness
and ladle lead into my
tired and weary bones

how do you know when it's time
time to let the painful optimism go?
because maybe they'll change
and maybe they already are

and maybe you're changing them
and how romantic would that be?
to satiate your burnt-out psyche
with his saliva, so refreshing

and it doesn't really hurt that bad
does it? and if it does, are you not in love with it all the more?
you who has born the blade centimeters from carotid puncture
and given only a toothy side-smile and a flush-ed glaze

why are you so scared of a pain as
common as heartbreak? with the tremors and vomit-
but no, they'll never come back to you
not in the way you want, so you cannot eat for fear of
losing that, too

baby, it's been almost a year
you're falling apart
barely scabbing at the raw-edged seam of it all
it's time to pack up, it's time to come home

summer awoke before dolores could beckon it,
the sun spreading the curtains wide and forcing
itself through like the hands of a man, always a man.
an assault on tired doe-ish eyes
and suddenly, she was painfully and ferociously alive-
she was in it!
in a hot hot world with a hot hot soul and cold hands,
she was gliding through lethal growing pains
a coquettish ice princess with torn-up stockings
and pen drawn down the back;
an homage to her nylon'd ancestors.

the winds of glossy-eyed change did push and shove her
halfway down the street
stumbling and scantily-clad and accented like the
swish-skirted cowgirls
with their purse-crooked elbows and long smiles
hair stuck to lipstick that smeared in
fine lines webbing cross'd pale skin
leaving strokes like varicose veins;
a funny game of magazine clipping and
selective medicating, to wash yourself into
a grown little girl.

waiting,
with bated breath
for the weather to change
for the shivering to shift
in meaning and direction
waiting,
with heavy heart
for the three-month chance
to find comfort in myself
to cup my lover's face
with dry hands and
steadied stance
once more

what a precious babe in my apple-chest
and how it cries and cries
to slip beneath my skin, it begs
for a tender allowance to die
the threes and fours of age and life
have found me cursed in hand
to find my sister-women living
in ways i never planned
and i wonder how, and when, and if
they knew their lives would go on
when i, in all my poisoned youth
never thought i'd survive this long
it spurns some idea of expiration
that i knew innately of my time passing
but i am not a jar of rot
curdled and cruel and foul-smelling
i am oven-fresh and bleached white-pure
while the bleating of my uncertain heart
goes on, and on, and on

it is truly something
to unveil a simmering reduction of
cranberry-soured hatred
in front of a national audience
with rows and rows of women sitting
on plaid couches
like little girls on a train
knees perched close together
hands clasped white and cold
silently begging for change
and it is truly something
to be raised fearing your own optimism
and now the fragments of hope grow further
apart in seed and in strength
is it really so much to ask
to see a long-haired shepherd
with gentle eyes and bright smile
guiding the patient lambs-
is it really so much to ask
for a woman to sit in the
tall-backed leather chair
just once in my little lifetime?

the blood ran cold
and steady as a thin red pole
down her thighs, her hands,
her toes webbed maroon
she held hope like a fragile star
burning her palms
and scarring her heart-
she knew it was her safest option-
she knew death was just around
that daunting corner
but nobody really tells you how
hard it is to rid yourself
so messily, so painfully
of everything you have always wanted
tearing a rib from her own chest and tossing it
tearfully into the cold black of the night
she sang both of them a lullaby
hoping it would soothe her eternally
sorry soul

sweetly-scented floral wreaths
mingling with humid dirt
he slides his hand up my thigh
i clutch the crucifix lasso-tied 'round my sore throat
i pray for god to save me
he tells me to save myself

i fear the darkness in my bedroom
i stumble to the side of the bed and pray
i pray for god to guide me
i fall into the bed frame and the scrap metal
forces its way into my skin
he tells me to heal myself

i pray to be his perfect girl
pretty and clean and well-rounded
but the devastation he entrusted me with
is a plague, a disease, incurable, wasting
and his reasoning seems unfounded

he tells me to save myself
he knows not what i need saving from
he knows not
for
if i could never be god
there is no way he could have ever been me
how could he?
he is simply another father figure
claiming your body is not bloating and stretching to carry the
weight of his sins
claiming that actually, he has no sins at all

did you know it would be like this
so torturous in shape
such a difficult series of spasms and coughs
the strangest shedding of all i held in my heart
all i deemed important had disappeared
i unloaded the groceries
i swept the driveway
i cleansed my mind
and nobody knew
and nobody condemned my behavior
but nobody praised it, either
i had no idea the finish line would come for us so early
i was not privy to your plans
did you think that this was for the best
to let me rot in silence?

how is it possible
that you took a stupid and girlish heart
glued to the frame of a starved and grating body
and made it feel so replenished
that it, in all of its profound skeletal frailty
for a single moment
could find meaning in the pitch-black'd darkness
and i could hold my own hand
kiss mine own shoulder
but still, i look to you through the crook'd neck
and turn of bone that betrays me in unspoken ways
i hope you sleep well at night when the moon does
its dripping down into the eyes and tangling of the lashes
even when you find weight in strange pockets like
saddlebags against hip and thigh, i do
because every bled 'til labour'd heart
blinks in spite of solace to see you disrupting their peaceful
eternal farewells with your moaning insomniac tendencies
they shimmer and pop and crust and die
and all that dust and sorrow,
all that dirt at the bottom of the lake
it pools at the corners of your upturn'd mouth
and i want to feel it
i want to hold it and mold it and tear at it with my
crumbling jawbone swollen and understand
exactly how you feel when you are alone

i cannot, i cannot, i cannot
speak on the ways in which my body
has been licked and split and beat
i walk sideways
down the ledge
all of me is aching
with the painful god-eyes watching
the only fleshy simulation to know
the tortures i swore into secrecy within
my spine's fragile ends
the bleating of my begging valves
my exhausted arteries
choking and spitting and sputtering as though
only grease is left inside me
even my lifeblood has changed in chemical form
from pure hatred, absolutely destroyed
to burn me, to burn me, to burn me
and it was so many years behind
it could have been left alone
but i stick my finger in that infected sore of a would-hole
every day and it still hurts, still hurts, still hurts

when i go to heaven
my mommy will be there
my father will hug me
they will say they know everything
and are proud of me anyways
the smaller self will sit sleeping on
the thick arm of a plush reading chair
so i may watch her live without
the pain inside her chest
who could want for
more than that?

no matter how i wish to go back
my laughter carries a tension
my bones are restrained
i cannot run as i once did
fear has finally turn'd me adult
ossified me into this uncomfortable form

my skin is peeling in delicate peony petals
my eyes sit a wide audience
their twin-image the only witness to the shedding
the blistering pain consumes me whole
it hurts to move

i called for you here
i wanted to show you who i have become
but you could not seem to bear it
and in the end
i am blazing
deoxygenated
finding wicked ways to emulate who i almost was
something wicked takes hold
shakes me daily,
crouches over me like a curse
nightly-
it suffocates me, my own pillow
my own sheet wrapped 'round my sweaty neck
the disease of those i look up to
the disease that claims all that i do
the disease

an apology appears due
she did not know
his tongue flicks and flames
mirrors moonlight
mirrored sideways
directly inside the pales of her eyes

she did not know he saw her
as an apple, how he bit
a pomegranate always with
digging and tearing and
horrifying verb after another
yelling and blood should
stain the same

she had put away the blade the bullet
knife and nicotine
driving with no seat-belt
crossing roads with eyes squeezed tight as limes
breathing so slow it was not breathing at all,
just dizzy white noise rivaling no one
only to fill one singular hole with the whole of evil

he said
to that little girl in her mind
that he loved her, as he
cradled so gentle he must have had children
maybe her age, maybe more
how could she have known
for he was too good at it all
and she was finally happy

she was a tenderly devoted darling
in kisses and braids and bread and wine
to pair lipstick with life
how a delicate lace garment
did drape as a silver curtain
and it had been a strong resistance
a french resemblance
froze her within a deviously devil'd
destruction of character
studying the trials of temptation as they
ruined her heart 'til it did rot
and could only be understood in autopsy

who knows if we'll make it through
the first sweating of the snow
but the question will forever remain
of what love could be beyond pain
if it would even feel lovely at all

what does it mean to suck
between my teeth and taste
blood lingering there
if the decay of mine skin has finally
caught up to my senses
can i not avoid it then?
and though the blisters have faded to
the glittering edge of a bubble popped
on hard-wood floors
the skin remains delicate and sore to touch
and to find a boy that presses just hard enough
to such that sharp breath
is it a curse, after all
my rounded face?
does it betray no pain?
does it preserve me as immortal in innocence
despite the ways i have been taut and twisted 'round
the fingers of so many disturbed by their own skin
praying to crawl inside of mine
what if they were successful
am i no longer my own?

i soaked it all up, the wet earth
i drank the humidity out of the air
and spit mosquitoes and crane flies
i didn't even know the name of that place
when i was inside it
when i showered with chilled water
and thought i may never think again
for having thought it all out and away
it hurt so badly
i wished for divine rearrangement
a blinding finger-tip to ease my scalp
to make it stop

i am not evil
i am not i know i am not
i soaked in the river for six days
and scorched on the stone for the
seventh, did not stare at the sun though
it stared at me did not drink from the
wine when i thirsted for warmth in the
winter and did not curl my tongue to speak
to a man for ninety days
did not eat
did not bleed
did not see the water reflected, brushed my
hair only at night and washed only in the rain
i am clean
i have cut my wrists ten-thousand times and
kindly escorted every gentle person from my life
until my brain my heart my stomach
they are all empty
but still, you stand before me
you regret me, call me evil
when all i am is sick